Witch's Kitchen

TABLE OF CONTENTS

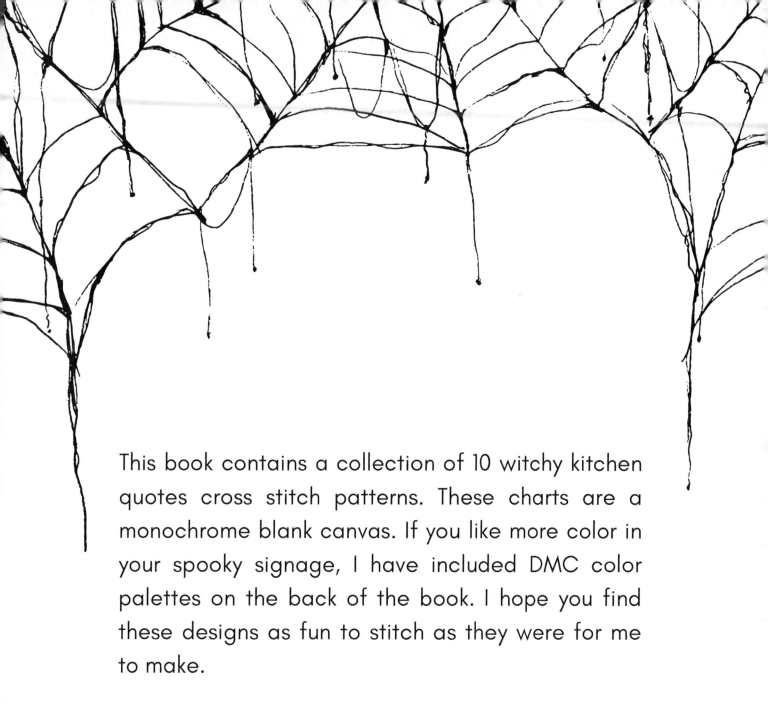

This book contains a collection of 10 witchy kitchen quotes cross stitch patterns. These charts are a monochrome blank canvas. If you like more color in your spooky signage, I have included DMC color palettes on the back of the book. I hope you find these designs as fun to stitch as they were for me to make.

Happy Stitching.

Maggie

To receive a free chart, please go to my site, StitchCabin.com, and click on FREE CHART.

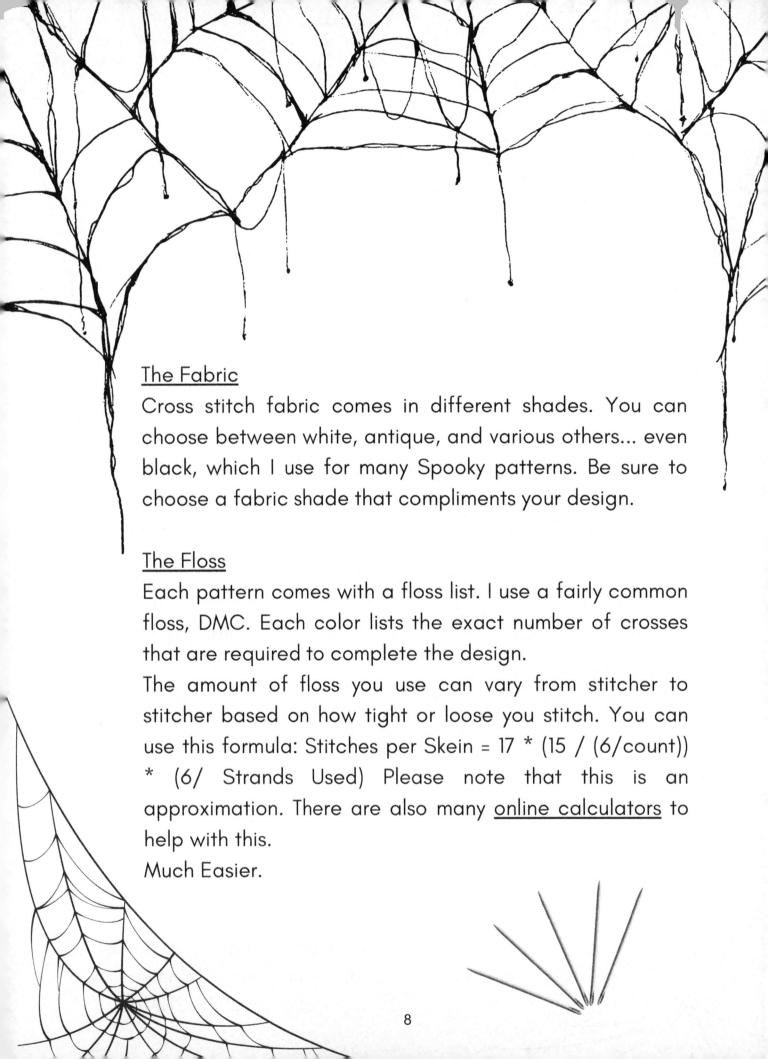

The Fabric

Cross stitch fabric comes in different shades. You can choose between white, antique, and various others... even black, which I use for many Spooky patterns. Be sure to choose a fabric shade that compliments your design.

The Floss

Each pattern comes with a floss list. I use a fairly common floss, DMC. Each color lists the exact number of crosses that are required to complete the design.

The amount of floss you use can vary from stitcher to stitcher based on how tight or loose you stitch. You can use this formula: Stitches per Skein = 17 * (15 / (6/count)) * (6/ Strands Used) Please note that this is an approximation. There are also many online calculators to help with this.

Much Easier.

Petite Stitches

Similar to a full cross stitch, a petite stitch is a small cross stitch which is made on the one quarter part of a square. As a result, a full square is made up of four small cross stitches instead of one big cross stitch. These little stitches are used for adding a more precise shape to a cross-stitch design. They are optional, however if you substitute full crosses for them you will have a more blocky pattern.

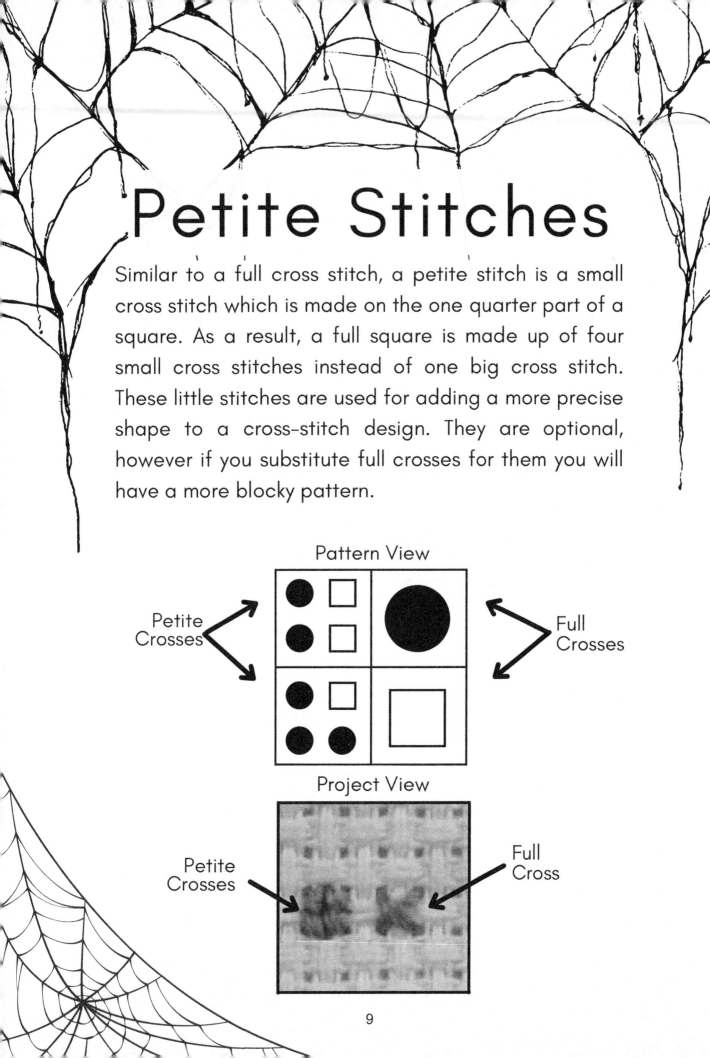

Pattern View

Petite Crosses

Full Crosses

Project View

Petite Crosses

Full Cross

Backstitch

Back Stitch is a line of straight stitches, made with a single embroidery thread. They are usually marked on a chart by a thick or colorful outline. Back Stitch is added after all of the cross stitches are complete. It is a finishing technique that can really bring your project to life. While they are optional, they can really alter how the final project looks.

Some stitchers Back Stitch through every square. For me, that is too tedious. I only do it for rounded corners. Most of the time, I prefer 2-3 squares.

Back Stitch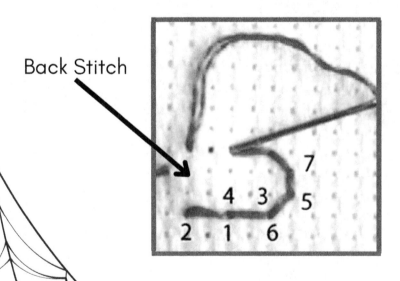

Example:
Bring the needle <u>up</u> at 1, <u>down</u> at 2, <u>up</u> at 3, <u>down</u> at 4, <u>up</u> at 5, <u>down</u> at 6, <u>up</u> at 7, and so forth. Notice that the same hole is used like in 1 and 4.

Project Size

All of the patterns in this book are measured at 14-count. You can size a project up or down by changing the count of the fabric.

To calculate the design size in inches, simply divide each dimension by 14 if using an Aida 14 fabric. (This is 14 crosses per inch) For example: If a design size is 126 x 154 crosses, you would divide 126 by 14 and 154 by 14, giving you a finished design that is 9" x 11" in size.

A common rule of thumb is to have at least 6 inches of fabric around your design to give you ample room for framing and matting. Be sure to factor that in when choosing your size of the fabric.

AIDA 14   AIDA 18

IN THIS KITCHEN WE USE MAGIC

On AIDA 14:
Design size: 103 x 117 stitches

Floss list for crosses

Use 2 strands of thread for cross stitch

N	Symbol		Number	Name	Full-Cross	Petit
1	●	◻	DMC 310	Black	3311	57

Floss list for backstitch

Use 1 strand of thread for backstitch

N	Line style	Number	Name	Units
1	——————	DMC 310	Black	1652

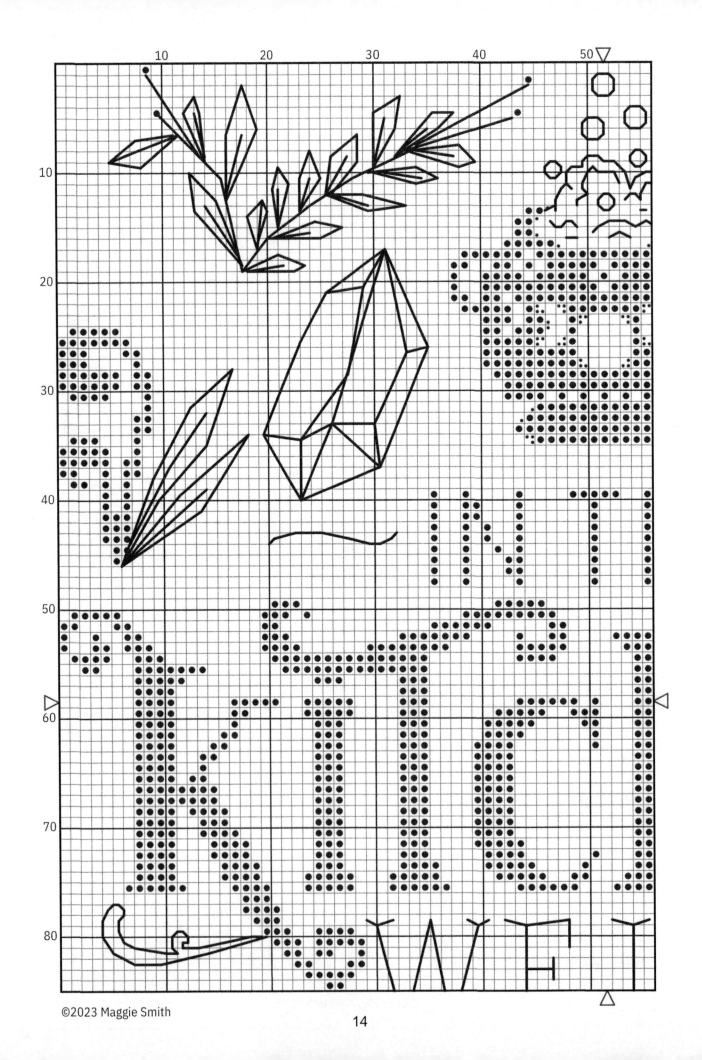

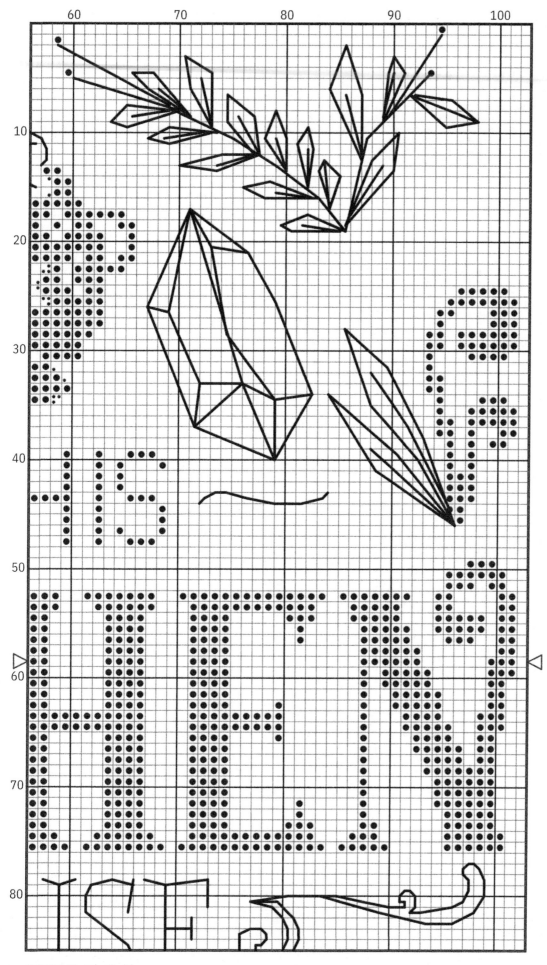

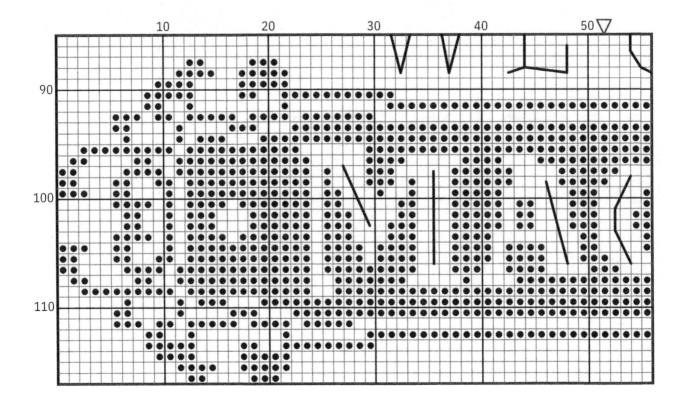

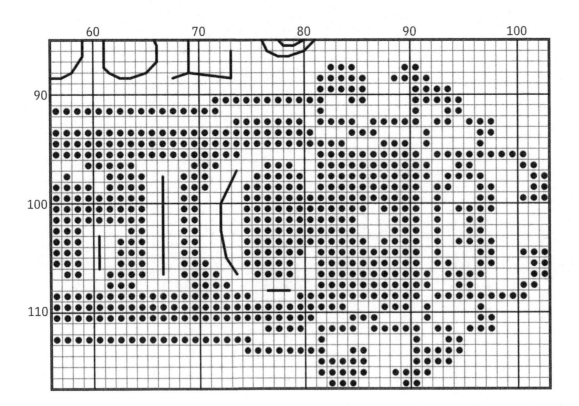

16

Witchin' in the Kitchen

On AIDA 14:
Design size: 106 x 172 stitches

Floss list for crosses

Use 2 strands of thread for cross stitch

N	Symbol		Number	Name	Full-Cross	Petite
1	●	◉	DMC 310	Black	7289.5	0

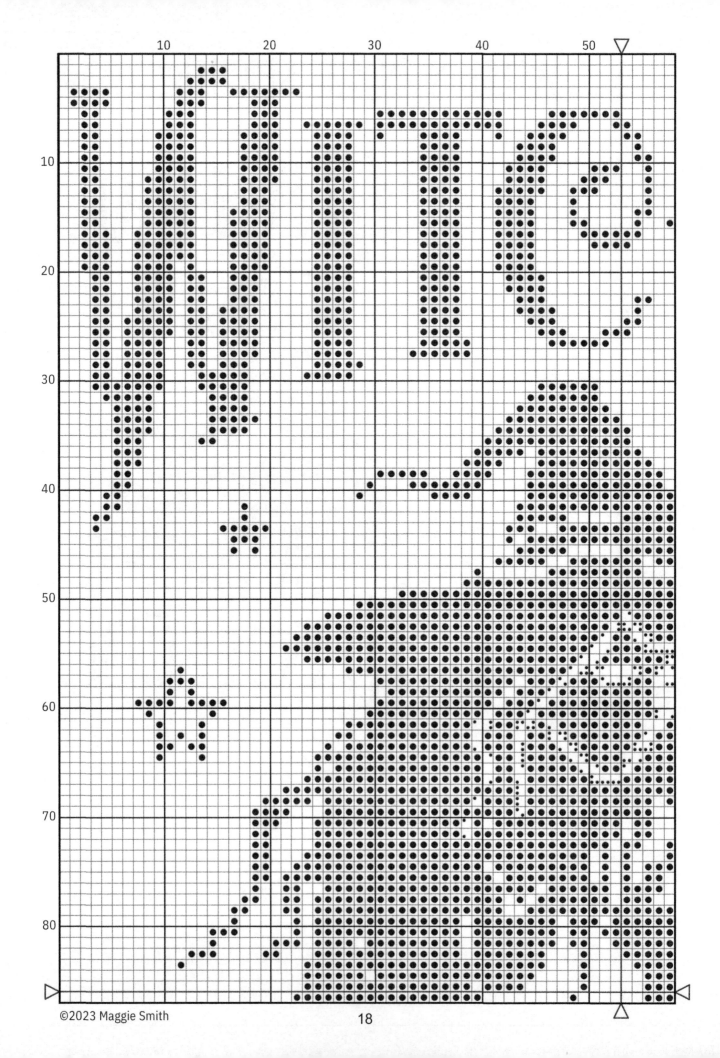

18

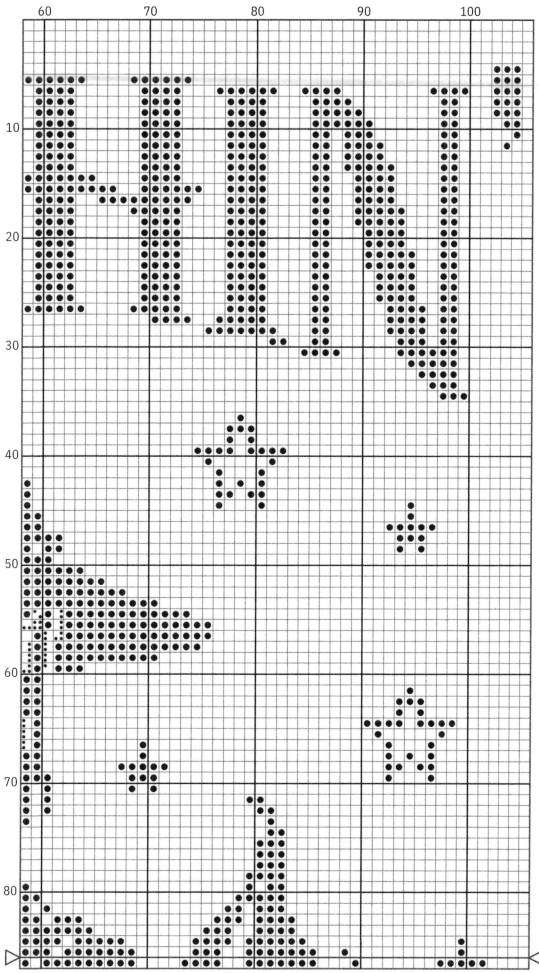

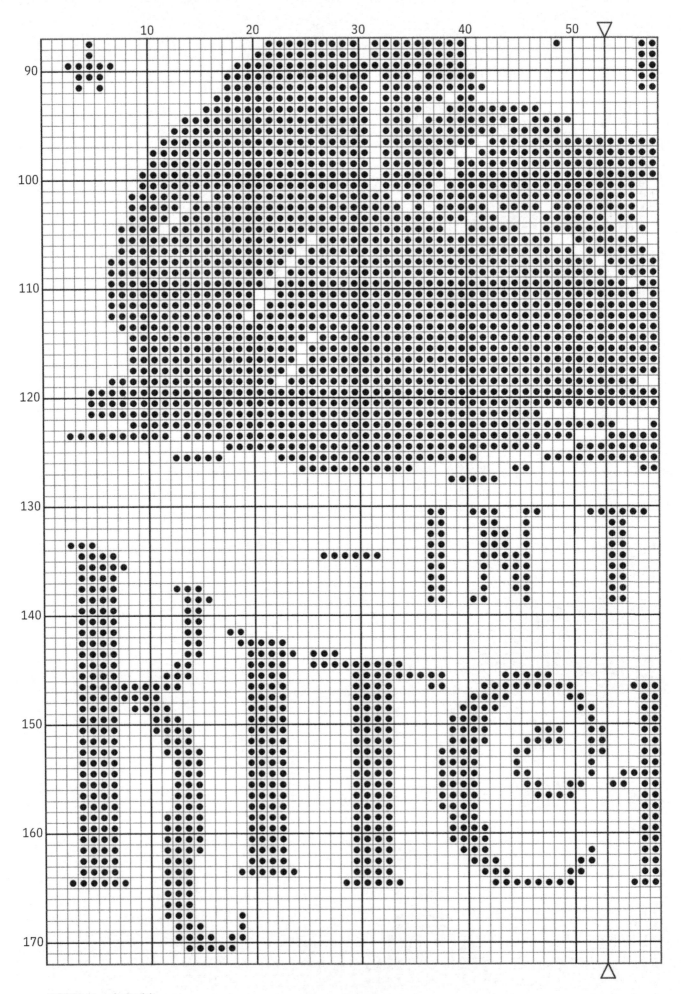

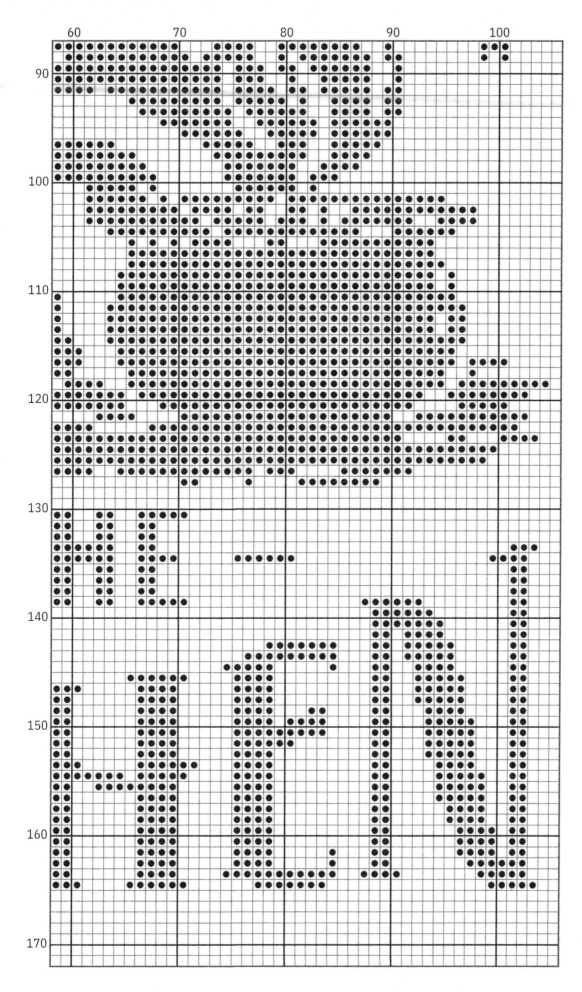

21

BLESS THIS MAGIC KITCHEN

On AIDA 14:
Design size: 100 x 123 stitches

Floss list for crosses

Use 2 strands of thread for cross stitch

N	Symbol		Number	Name	Full-Cross	Petite
1	●	◐	DMC 310	Black	3091	0

Use 1 strand of thread for backstitch

N	Line style	Number	Name	Units
1	————	DMC 310	Black	1443

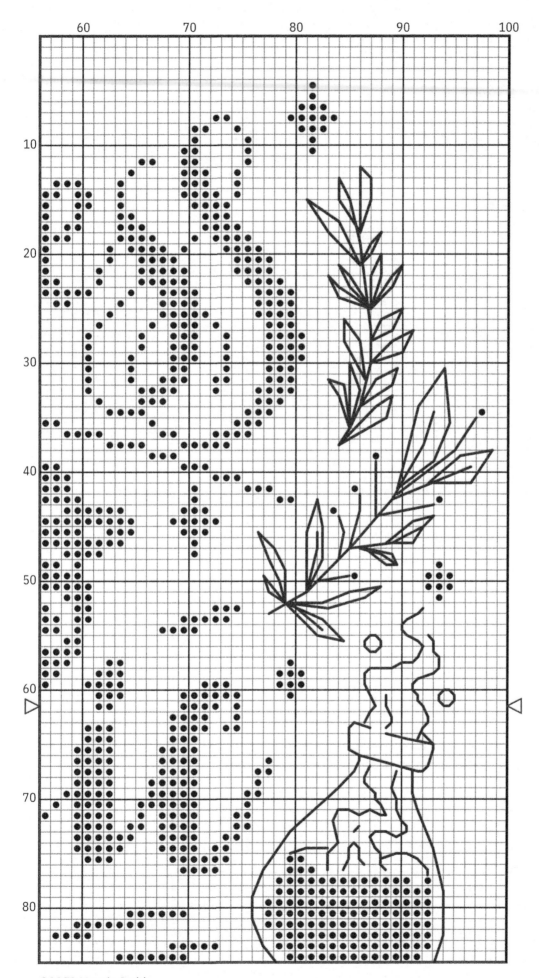

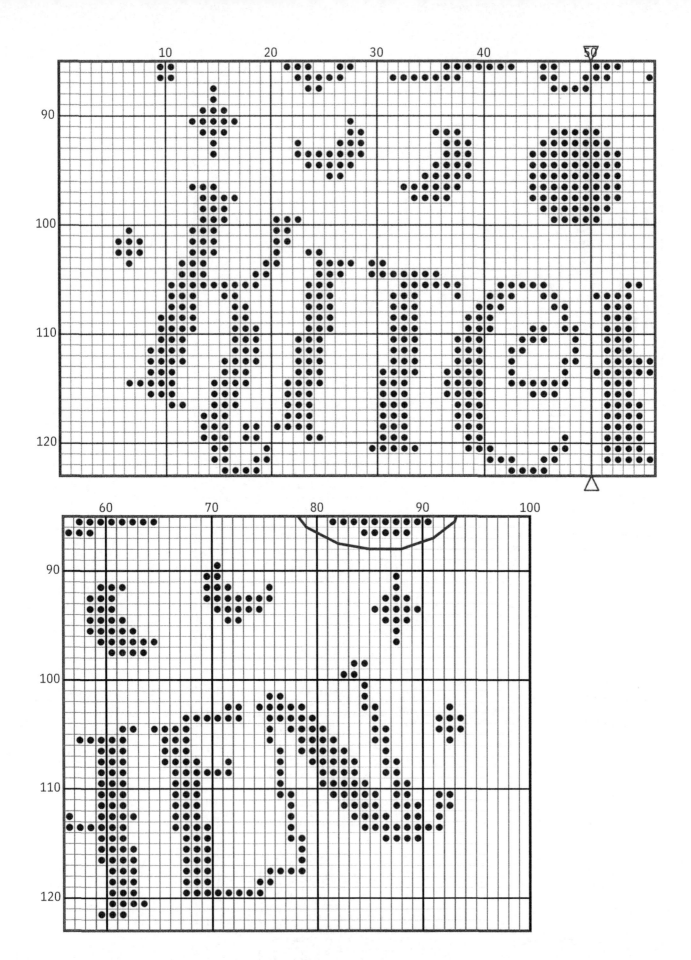

On AIDA 14:

Design size: 111 x 154 stitches

Floss list for crosses

Use 2 strands of thread for cross stitch

N	Symbol	Number	Name	Full-Cross	Petite
1	● ◐	DMC 310	Black	5828	0

Use 1 strand of thread for backstitch

N	Line style	Number	Name	Units
1	———	DMC 310	Black	384

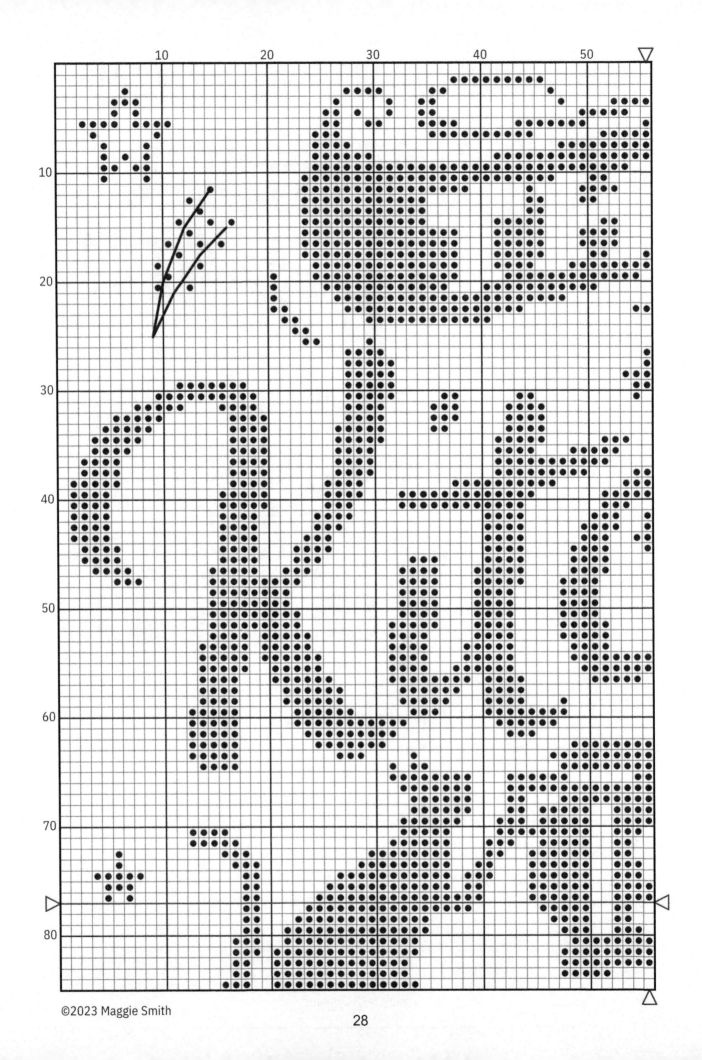

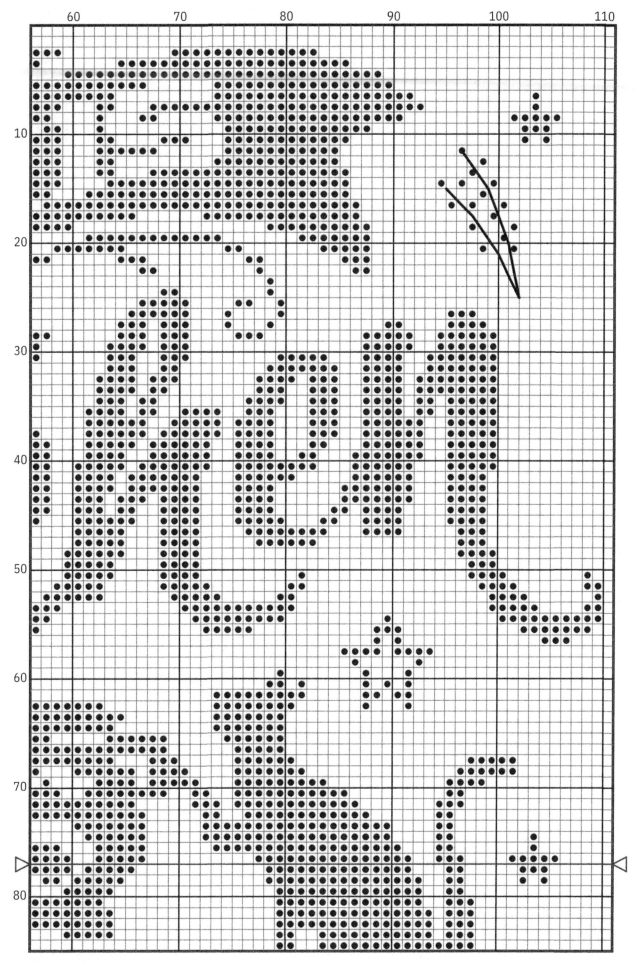

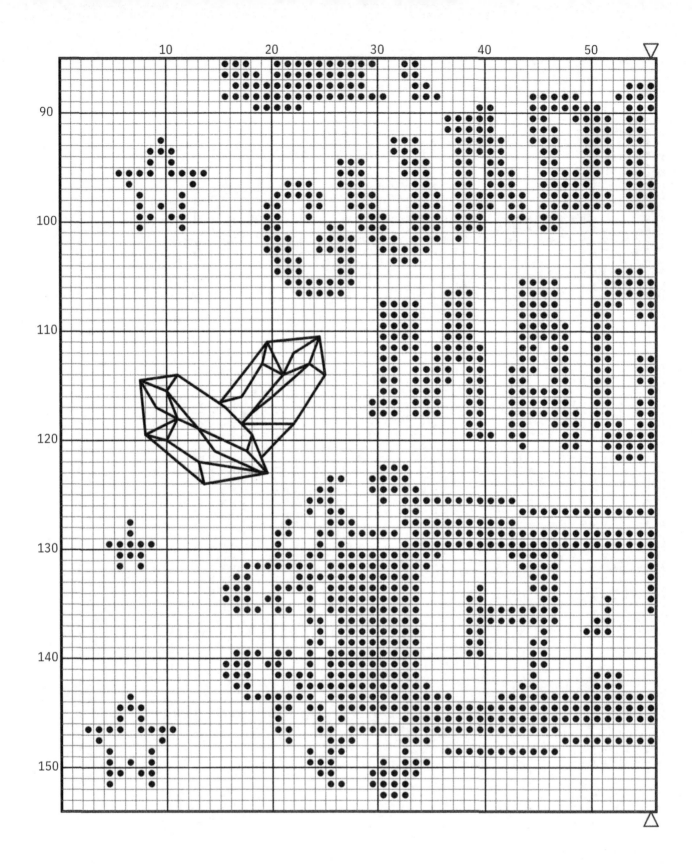

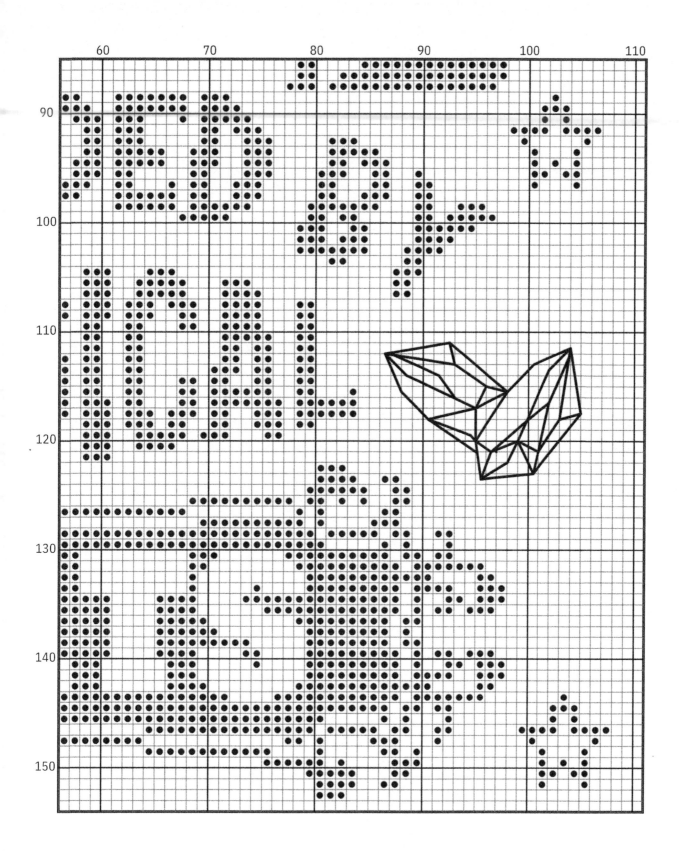

WELL BEHAVED CHILDREN WELCOME

On AIDA 14:
Design size: 112 x 98 stitches

Floss list for crosses

Use 2 strands of thread for cross stitch

N	Symbol	Number	Name	Full-Cross	Petite
1	● ◯	DMC 310	Black	2159.5	0

Use 1 strand of thread for backstitch

N	Line style	Number	Name	Units
1	——————	DMC 310	Black	1617

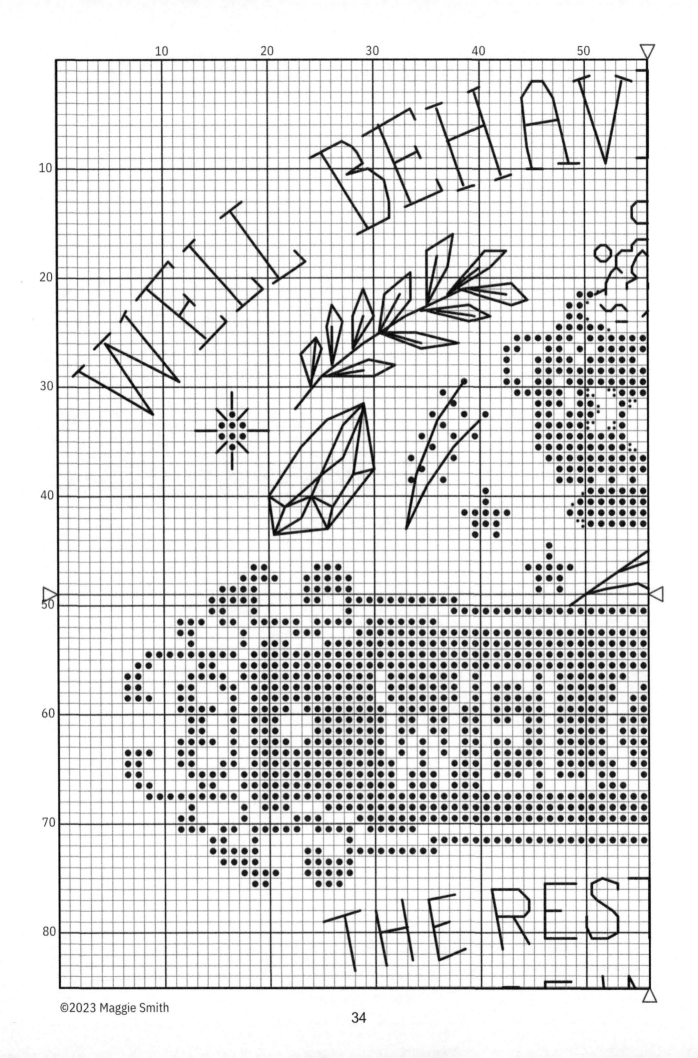

34

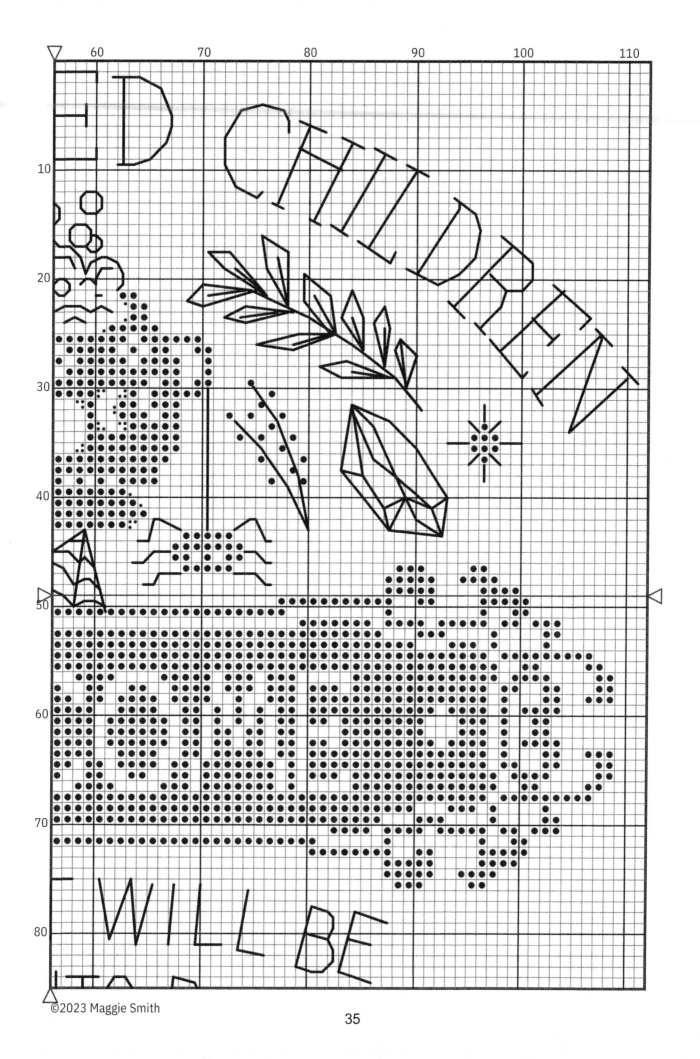

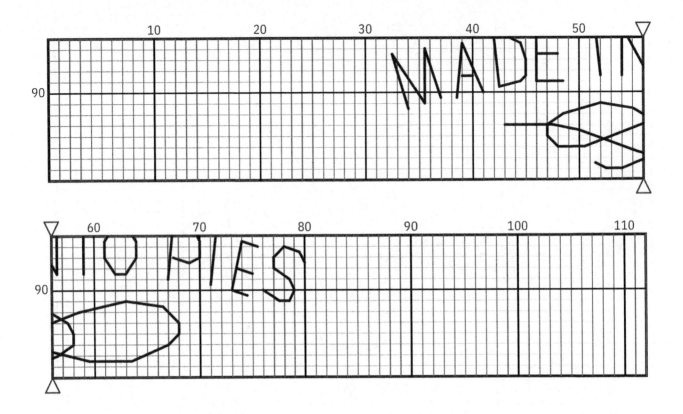

On AIDA 14:
Design size: 99 x 122 stitches

Floss list for crosses

Use 2 strands of thread for cross stitch

N	Symbol	Number	Name	Full-Cross	Petite
1	● ◯	DMC 310	Black	2653.5	0

Use 1 strand of thread for backstitch

N	Line style	Number	Name	Units
1	——	DMC 310	Black	1996

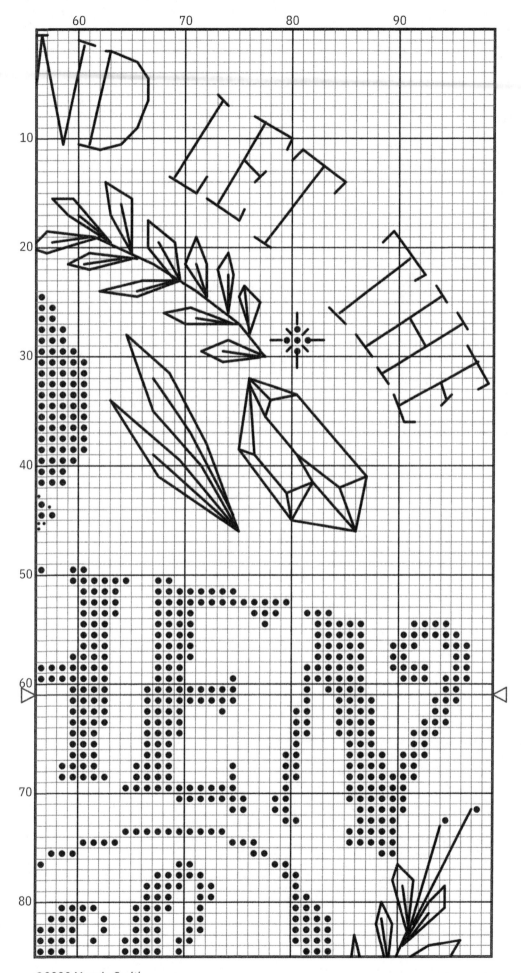

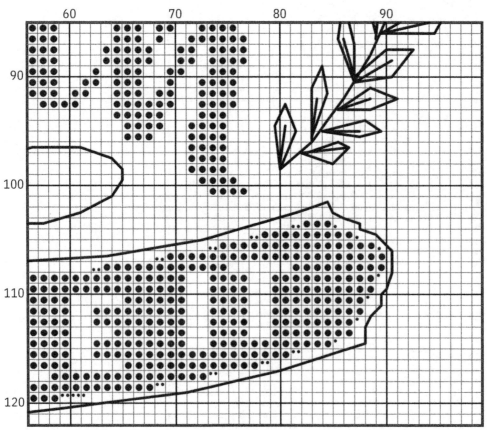

My Kitchen is For Dancing

On AIDA 14:

Design size: 160 x 205 stitches

Floss list for crosses

Use 2 strands of thread for cross stitch

N	Symbol		Number	Name	Full-Cross	Petite
1	●	◐	DMC 310	Black	8187	0

Use 1 strand of thread for backstitch

N	Line style	Number	Name	Units
1	———	DMC 310	Black	251

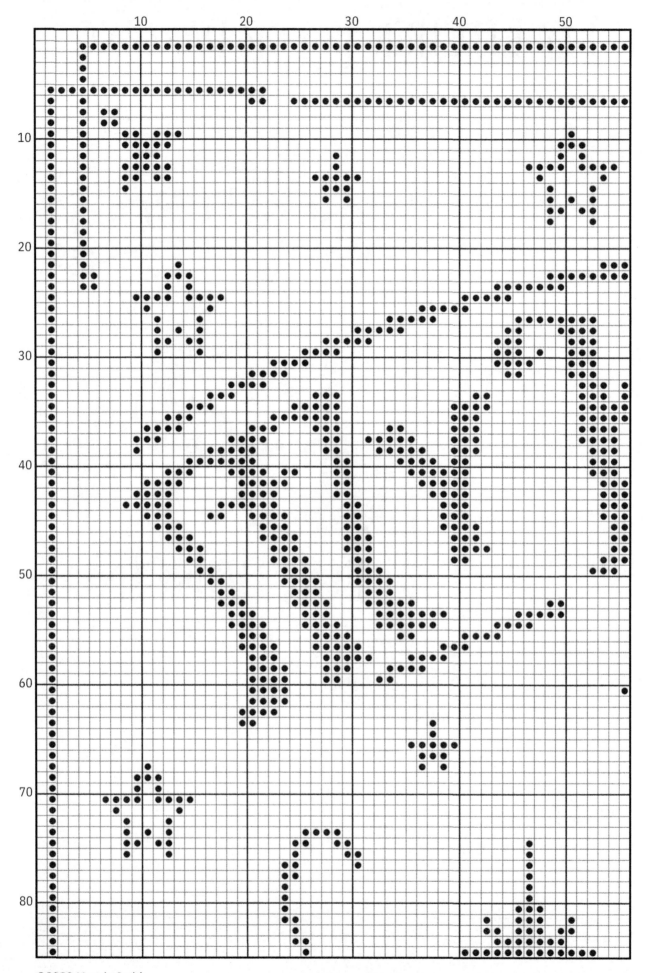

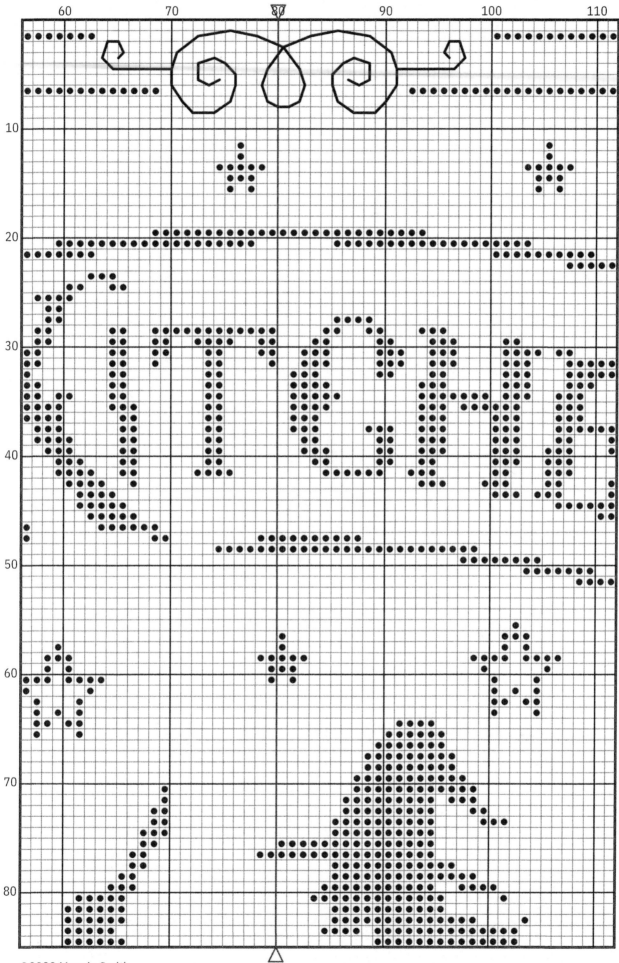

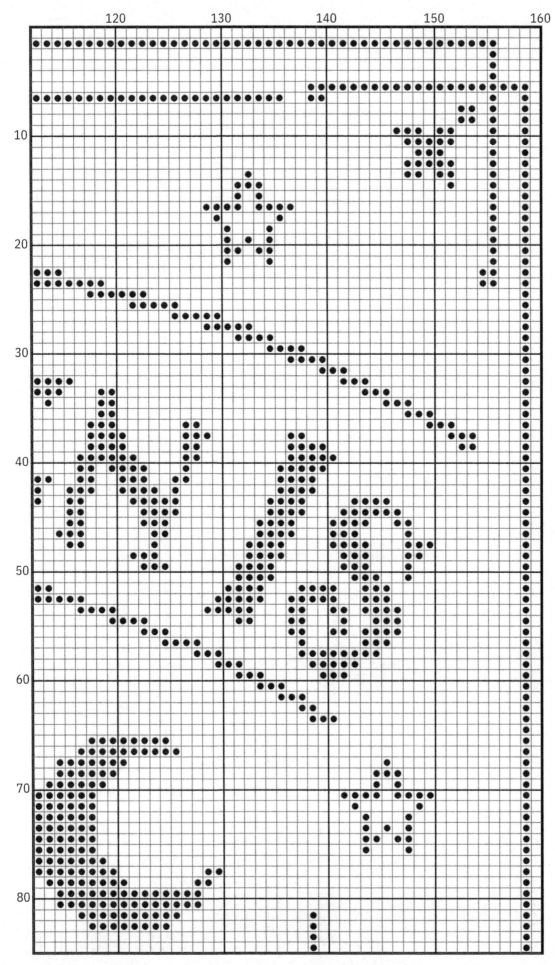

44

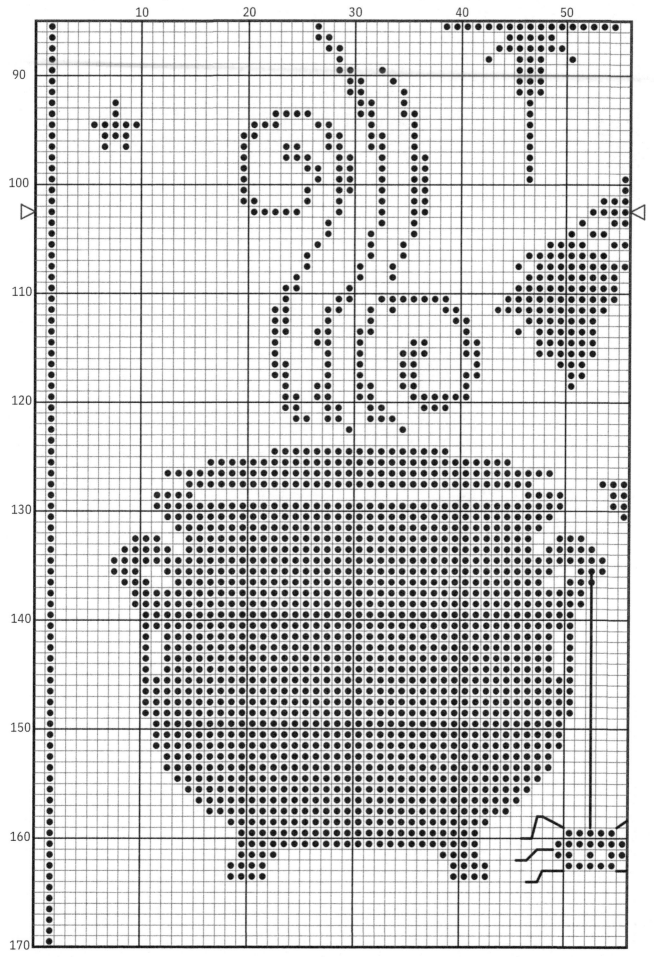

45

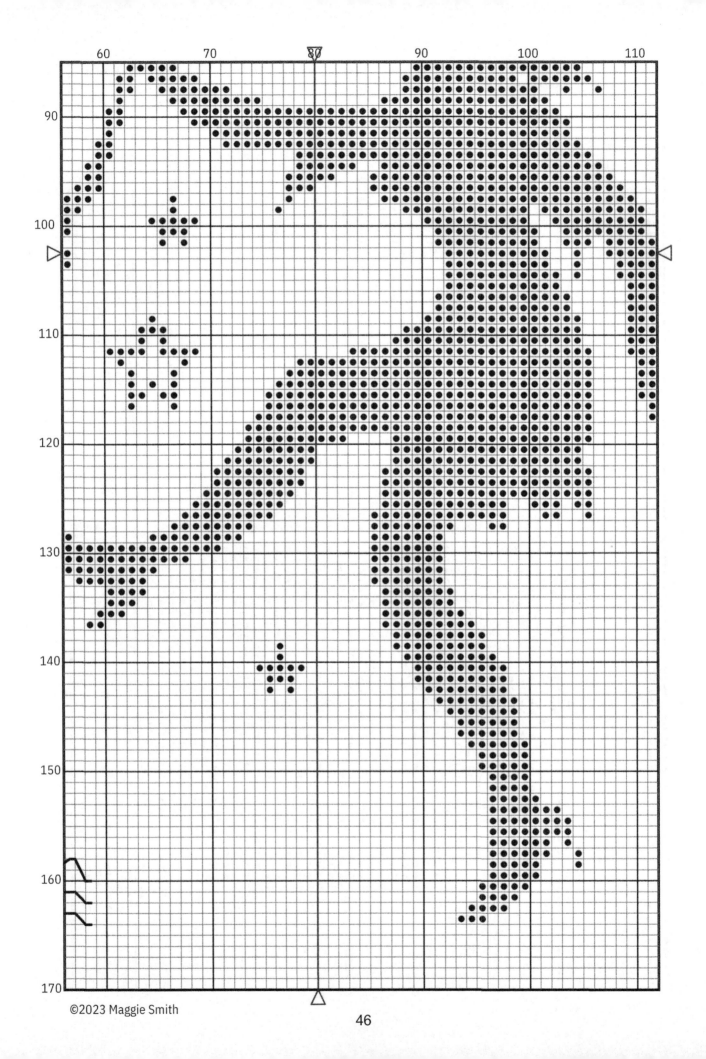

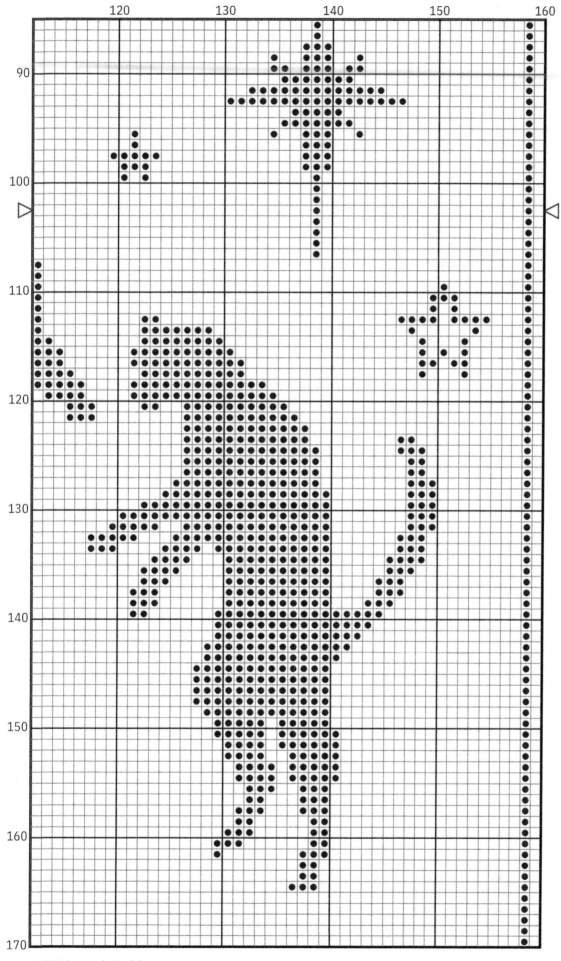

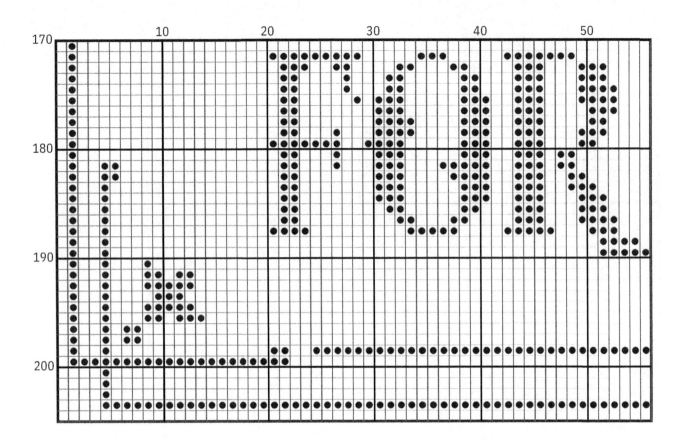

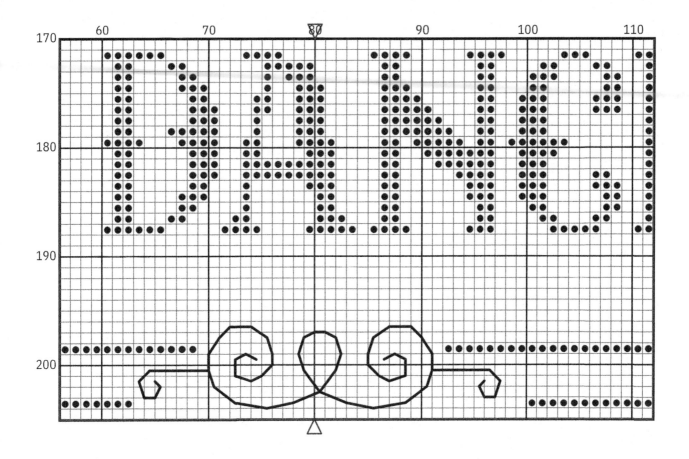

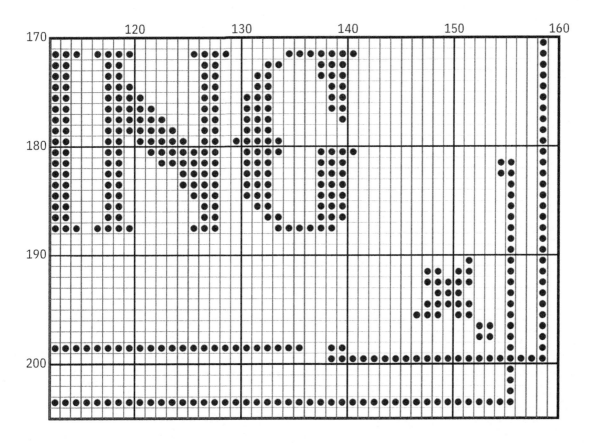

49

On AIDA 14:
Design size: 112 x 150 stitches

Floss list for crosses

Use 2 strands of thread for cross stitch

N	Symbol	Number	Name	Full-Cross	Petite
1	● ◉	DMC 310	Black	4610	0

Use 1 strand of thread for backstitch

N	Line style	Number	Name	Units
1	——	DMC 310	Black	774

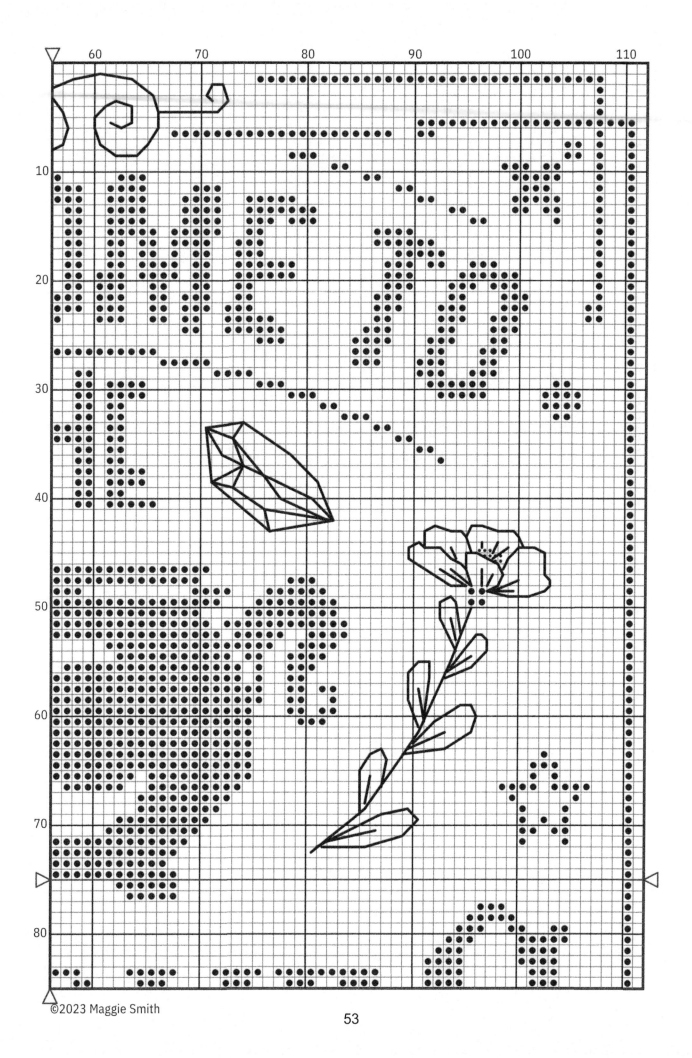

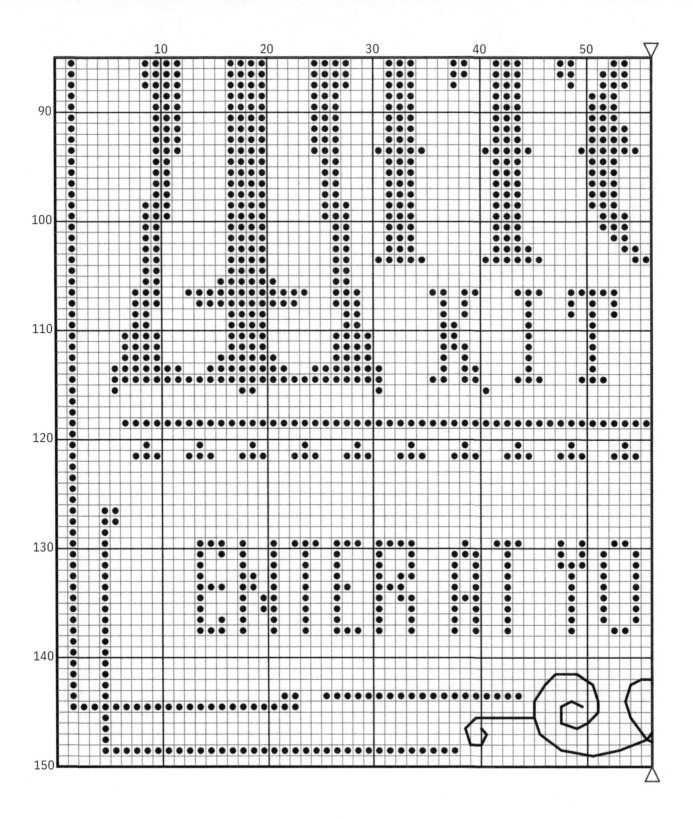

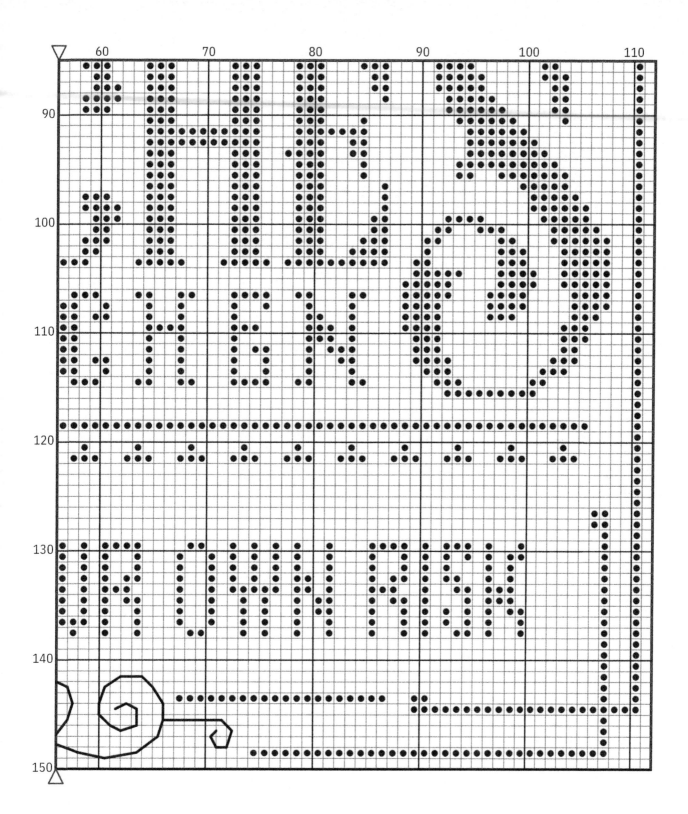

On AIDA 14:
Design size: 110 x 172 stitches

Floss list for crosses

Use 2 strands of thread for cross stitch

N	Symbol		Number	Name	Full-Cross	Petite
1	●	◐	DMC 310	Black	7314	0

Use 1 strand of thread for backstitch

N	Line style	Number	Name	Units
1	——	DMC 310	Black	301

58

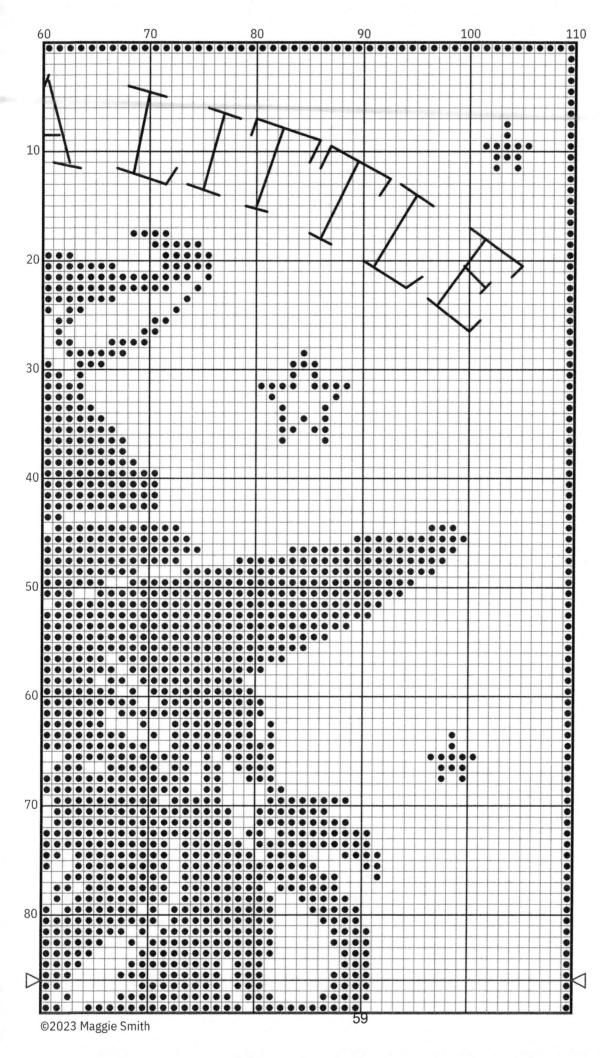

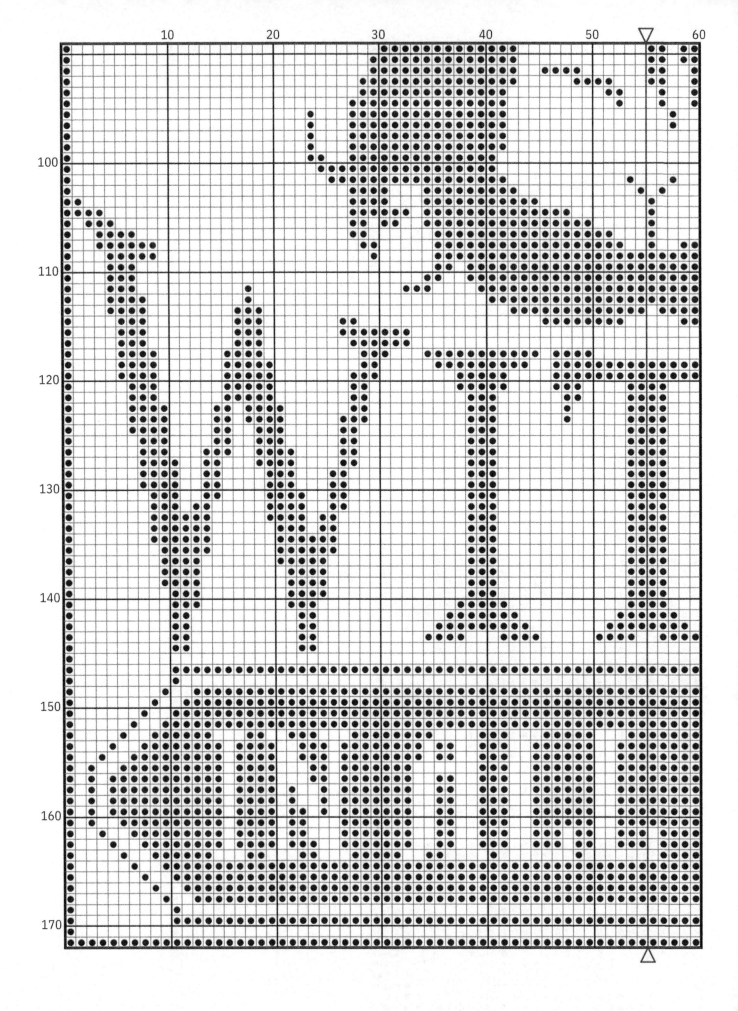

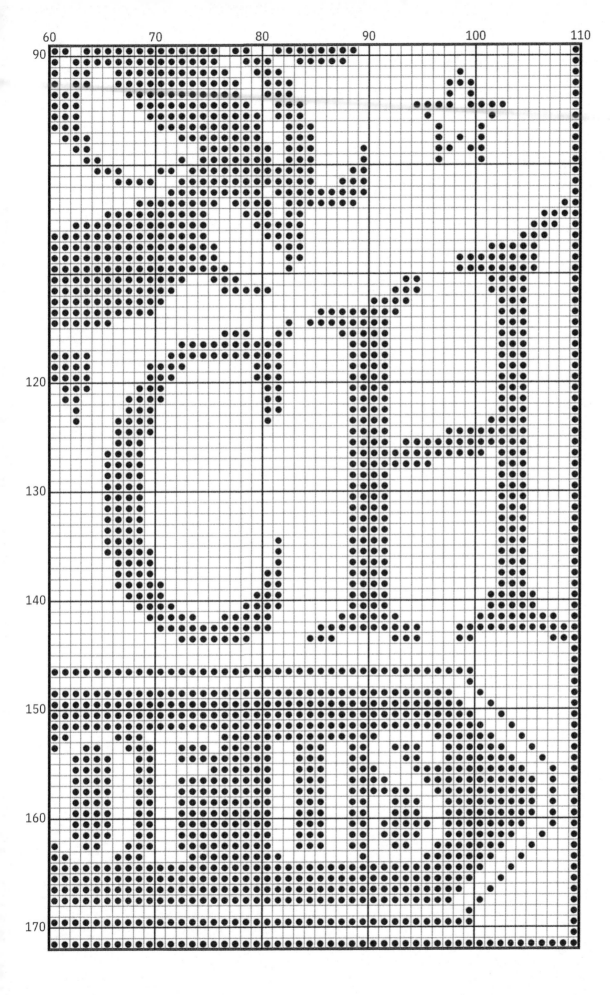

IF I HAVE TO STiR It IT'S HOMEMADE

On AIDA 14:
Design size: 172 x 123 stitches

Floss list for crosses

Use 2 strands of thread for cross stitch

N	Symbol		Number	Name	Full-Cross	Petite
1	●	◓	DMC 310	Black	8129	0

Use 1 strand of thread for backstitch

N	Line style	Number	Name	Units
1	——————	DMC 310	Black	175

©2023 Maggie Smith
63

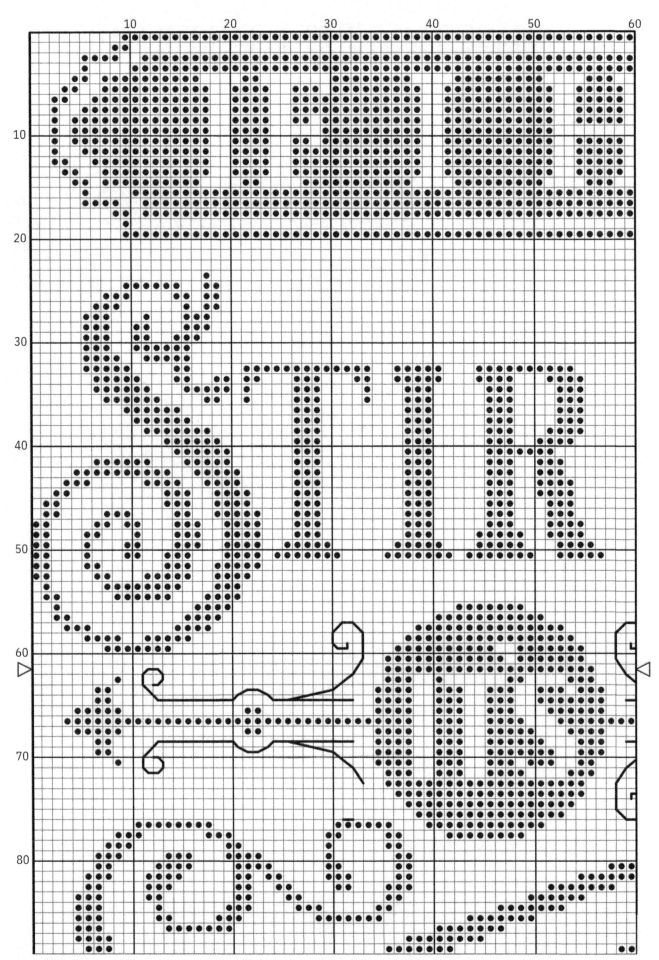

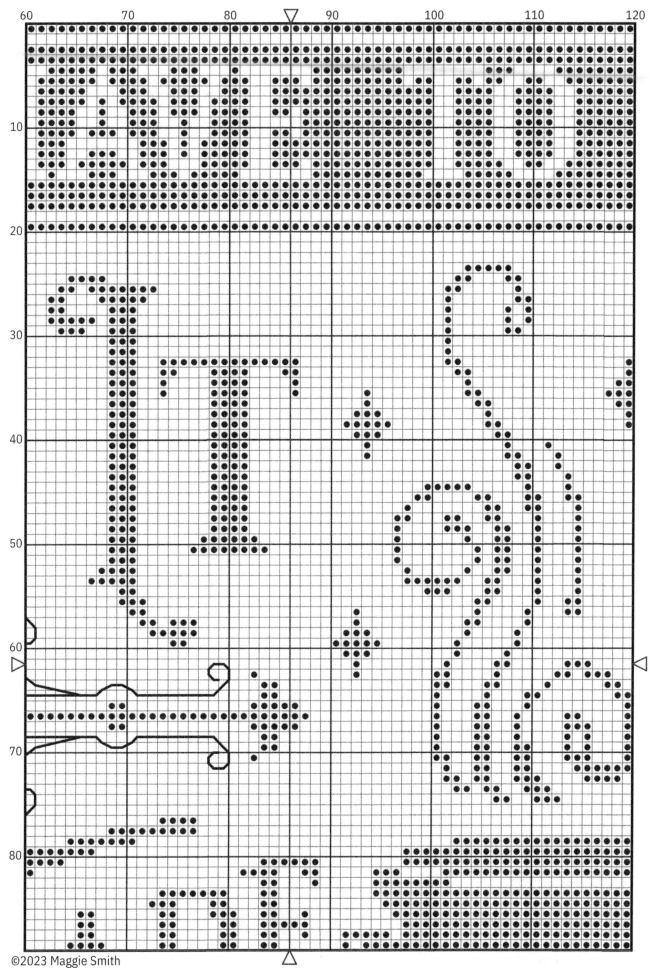

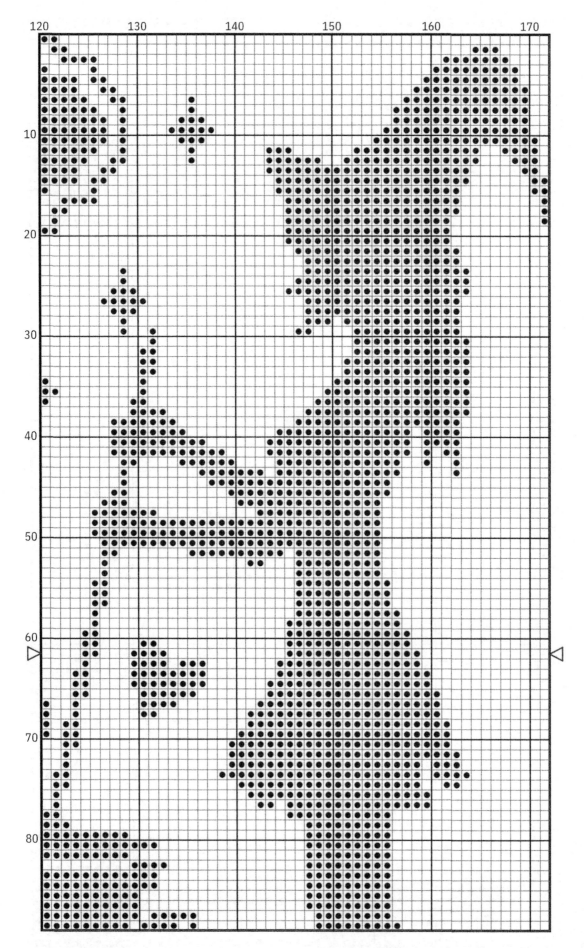

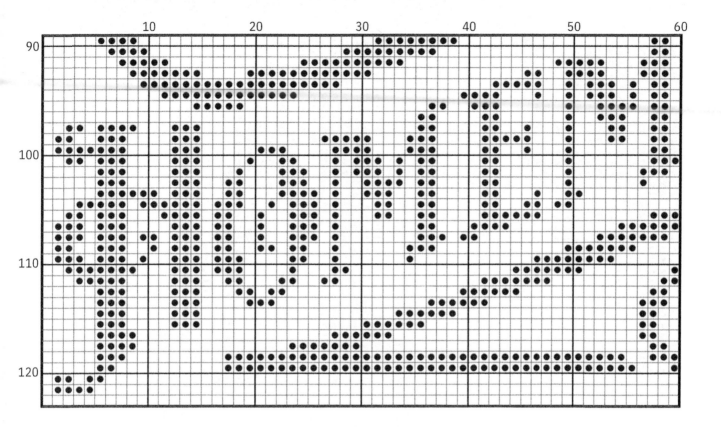

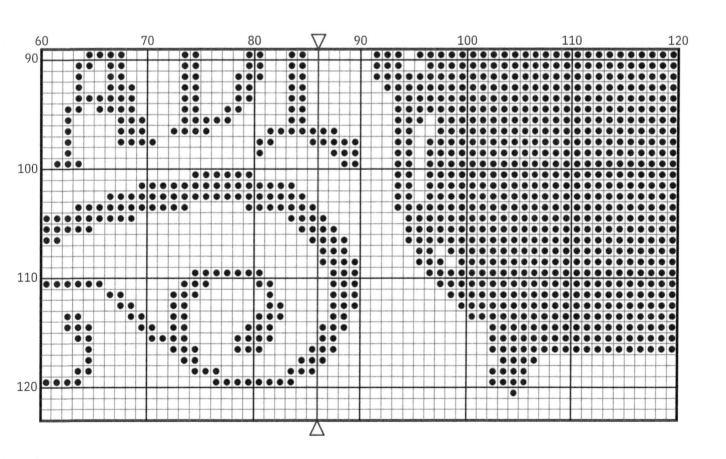

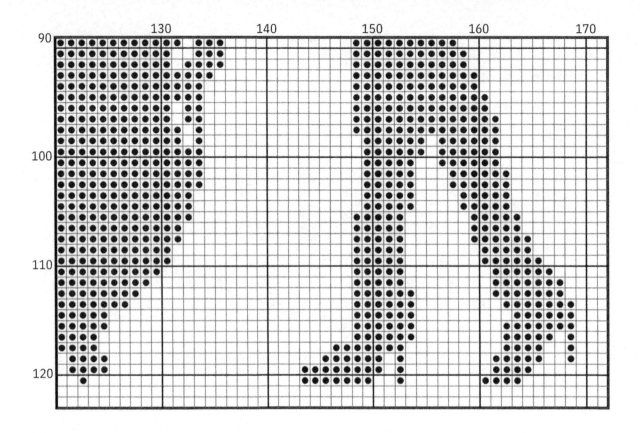

Printed in Great Britain
by Amazon

41169673R00040